She Never Looked Back

Margaret Mead in Samoa

by Sam and Beryl Epstein
illustrated by Victor Juhasz

Coward, McCann & Geoghegan, Inc. / New York

Library of Congress Cataloging in Publication Data

Epstein, Samuel. She never looked back.

Bibliography: p.

SUMMARY: A brief biography of the well-known
anthropologist concentrating on her first important
studies in Samoa in the mid-1920's.

1. Mead, Margaret, 1901–1978—Juvenile literature.
2. Anthropologists—United States—Biography—Juvenile
literature.   3. Ethnology—Samoan Islands—Juvenile
literature. [1. Mead, Margaret, 1901–1978
2. Anthropologists.   3. Ethnology—Samoan Islands]
I. Epstein, Beryl Williams, joint author.
II. Juhasz, Victor.   III. Title.

GN21.M36E67   301.2′092′4 [92]   78-31821   ISBN 0-698-30715-1

For Hildy and Dick Lockridge

ACKNOWLEDGMENTS

The authors wish to express their gratitude to the late Dr. Margaret Mead for her encouragement and for generously making available to them material from her own files; and to Dr. Rhoda Metraux, Dr. Mead's long-time associate, for her advice and suggestions during the preparation of this book. Grateful acknowledgment is also made to the Ambassador and First Secretary of the Samoan Permanent Commission to the U. N.

CONTENTS

1/ Kava Ceremony

It was the hour for drinking *kava* in the little village of Vaitogi on one of the Samoan Islands of the South Pacific. The blazing tropical sun had dropped low in the sky. A faint breeze rattled the leaves of the coconut palms and the breadfruit trees. The children, waking up from their afternoon's sleep, had wandered toward the rocky shore to swim or bathe. The men of the village were gathering as usual in the *faletele*, the guest house, but today's session there would be a special occasion.

Today the kava would be served by the gray-eyed white-skinned young woman who had recently come to Samoa from far beyond the sea. Their Samoan name for her was Makelita. The name on her United States passport was Margaret Mead.

Earlier that same year of 1925, back home in New York, twenty-three-year-old Margaret Mead had faced a difficult examination for her doctorate degree. The subject had been anthropology, the study of human cultures—people's customs, their beliefs, their ways of life. She had done very well that day. Now she felt as if she were facing another kind of examination and she didn't know whether she would pass or not. She hoped very much that she would.

Vaitogi's principal chief, Ufuti, had told the villagers to treat Makelita as if she were his daughter. He had even given her the same kind of title he'd given his own daughter. He had made her a *taupou*, a ceremonial princess. So Chief Ufuti and all his many relatives would be shamed if Makelita failed to do well today. And the chief who had taught her the kava-serving ceremony would also be shamed if she didn't perform it properly.

With Fa'amotu, Chief Ufuti's nineteen-year-old daughter, Margaret crossed the open space in the middle of the village. Fa'amotu was black-haired and had light brown skin. She wore the Samoans' wraparound skirt, called a *lavalava,* and a sleeveless bodice above it that left her arms and shoulders bare. There were garlands of flowers and leaves around her neck, her wrists, and her ankles. She moved with a stately grace.

Margaret, shorter and more slender, wore one of the simple cotton dresses she had brought from home. Usually her step was so quick and light that her curly brown hair bounced up and down as she walked. Today her hair lay smooth. She was approaching the guest house with all the dignity she could manage.

The faletele was larger than the other houses in Vaitogi, but like them in all other ways. Its floor of small coral pebbles was raised above the ground on a stone platform. It had no permanent walls. Its roof, a high cone of sugarcane thatch, was supported only by widely spaced poles. Blinds made of overlapping mats could be lowered between those poles in bad weather. Now they were tied up to the rafters out of sight. Margaret's serving of the kava—like most events of her life in Vaitogi—could be seen by the whole village.

8

When she and Fa'amotu entered, the men were already there, seated cross-legged on the mats covering the pebble floor. Each of the chiefs had his own place at the base of one of the roof-supporting poles. Near him sat his assistants, his "talking chiefs," who made speeches for him and carried out his ceremonial duties. Men without any chiefly rank sat in other parts of the house, with no poles at their backs. All wore lavalavas of brightly printed cloth, fastened at the waist. Their upper bodies were bare and glistening with oil.

Margaret and Fa'amotu were led to their places near the big wooden kava bowl standing on its own stubby legs. Fa'amotu folded herself down into the cross-legged position. Margaret wished she could do it as gracefully. But once seated, she remembered to hold her back straight and erect.

They had entered in silence. For them to have spoken before they sat down would have been a great discourtesy. It would have meant that the men had to look up at them. But now it was time to repeat the polite phrases of greeting.

Margaret spoke first, as a visitor to Vaitogi. She tried to raise and lower her voice with the proper Samoan inflection, in a kind of singsong. In certain words she put in the little gulp that was as much a part of the Samoan language as any other sound. (Language experts call this a glottal stop. When Samoan words are written it is shown by an apostrophe, as in Fa'amotu.)

A quick glance from the chief who had taught her told Margaret she had done well.

Then Fa'amotu greeted her father's guests and began to prepare their drink. She put whitish shreds of kava-bush roots into the big bowl,

9

added water, and stirred. The men watched her, talking among themselves. Margaret sat motionless, arms folded as she had been taught. Even when a fly settled on her nose she didn't raise a hand to brush it away.

She kept her eyes on the coconut shell beside the kava bowl. That was the cup in which the kava would be served, each man drinking out of it in turn. For each man it would be called by a different name, in his honor, and the names would be announced in order, beginning with the cup-name of the visiting chief.

Finally Fa'amotu began to remove the kava root from the liquid, using a whisk of thin green strands of hibiscus bark that caught and held the shreds. The process took a long time. The fly on Margaret's nose moved to her cheek and back again.

At last the grayish liquid in the bowl was perfectly clear. One of Chief Ufuti's talking chiefs announced that the kava was ready.

All the other men in the room immediately began a loud rhythmic clapping. Over that deafening noise the talking chief shouted the cup-name of the visiting chief.

Margaret rose to her feet. Her body ached from holding its difficult position, but the persistent fly had fled as she moved. She stood before the kava bowl while Fa'amotu dipped the coconut shell into it, and held the filled cup out to her. Margaret curved her right hand into the shell's shape before she took it. Turning slowly, she walked toward the visiting chief.

Suppose she stumbled? she was thinking. Or suppose an insect fell into the cup?

10

Then she was standing before the imposing old man. She placed her left hand behind her back, palm out. With her right hand she raised the cup high over her head. She held it there briefly before sweeping it low to the floor before the chief. He accepted it from her.

Margaret straightened up from her bow. She hadn't stumbled. There was no insect in the cup.

The chief drank the sharp-tasting kava in small sips. He spilled the last few drops on the floor, according to Samoan custom, and handed the cup back to her. She returned to the kava bowl so that Fa'amotu could refill it for another chief whose cup-name was now being called.

Margaret glanced quickly around the room. Since she knew few of the men, and none of their cup-names, she had to depend on the signal that had been arranged to help her.

One man was clapping his hands gently. That meant the cup-name that had just been called belonged to him. She took the newly filled cup from Fa'amotu and moved toward him, to repeat once more the formal gestures of presenting it.

One by one she served the chiefs. Then it was the turn of the talking chiefs. For them the serving ceremony was a little simpler, but it too had to be carried out with absolute precision.

Finally the cup-name of every man in the guest house had been called, and every man had been served. Chief Ufuti, as host, had received the final cup. When he spilled its last drops on the floor, and Margaret had brought the cup back to its place at the kava bowl, her ordeal was over.

As she and Fa'amotu left the house, another round of loud clapping

11

told her she had not shamed her teacher and Chief Ufuti and her whole new Samoan family.

She hoped the days she was spending in the village of Vaitogi would help prepare her for the work she had come so far to do.

That work would make Margaret Mead, almost overnight, one of the best-known anthropologists in the world.

2/ "She Never Looked Back!"

As a little girl Margaret Mead decided she would like to marry a minister and have six children. But that answered only half of the question about what she would do when she grew up.

Her grandmother had taught school while she brought up Margaret's father. Her mother, Emily Fogg Mead, had gone on with her own work after Margaret, her younger brother, and two younger sisters were born. So Margaret took for granted that she too would have both a career and a family.

She thought of becoming a sociologist like her mother, who studied the community life of various groups of people. She thought of being a psychologist, of studying the mind and how it controls human behavior. She thought of other possibilities too—the law, politics, and writing.

One subject that didn't interest her much was economics, which her professor father, Edward Sherwood Mead, taught at the University of Pennsylvania in Philadelphia. But she did agree with one thing Professor Mead often told her.

"Adding to the world's store of knowledge is the most important thing a human being can do," he said.

In her senior year at Barnard College in New York City, Margaret decided that she could best add to the world's store of knowledge by becoming a psychologist. She planned to take advanced work in that field after her graduation and her marriage to Luther Cressman, the young man she had fallen in love with while still in high school. Luther was studying to be a minister and he too thought it would be fine to have six children. Margaret Mead's life seemed neatly settled.

But that same year Margaret took a course in anthropology which was offered only to the most distinguished Barnard seniors. Her professor was Franz Boas, a stern-looking old man who had spent years with the Eskimos and with the Kwakiutl Indians of British Columbia. He had wanted to learn what their different cultures had been before the first white man came into their lands. Now he was training young American anthropologists to learn about the American Indians and their ancient ways of life.

"You can see why his work is so important," Margaret told Luther and her friends. "Soon not a single Indian will be left who can remember a buffalo hunt! But if anthropologists go out into the field now, while there are still Indians alive who remember such things, we can find out about their ancient ways before they are all lost forever."

"But who wants to know about the old ways of primitive savages?" someone once asked her.

"They are not 'savages'!" Margaret said. "An anthropologist calls certain people primitive, but that just means their culture doesn't include a written history and a knowledge of modern science. Of course, they live differently from the way we do, because they've learned different things. But they and we are all human beings who have to solve the same basic problems: how to get food, how to organize families and groups so they get along together, how to bring up children so they'll know what is expected of them when they're grown up. And if we learn how primitive people solved these problems, we'll know a lot more about ourselves and about what we call 'human nature.' "

In the fall of 1923 Margaret and Luther were married. She wasn't called Mrs. Cressman, however. She was still Margaret Mead.

"Women should keep their own identity," she insisted to anyone who questioned her about that. And Luther agreed with her.

They shared the housework in their tiny New York apartment. They both had part-time jobs while they continued their studies. Every week they tried to invent some new ways to cook hamburger, the cheapest meat they could buy.

Luther took courses in sociology because he thought an understanding of human relations would make him a better minister. Margaret was hurrying to finish her work in psychology because she had changed her mind about her career. She had decided to be an anthropologist.

She had discussed her future with Ruth Benedict, Professor Boas's assistant, who would become an outstanding anthropologist herself and Margaret's lifelong friend. And she had become convinced, as she explained years later, that "anthropology had to be done *now*. Other things could wait."

By the summer of 1924 she wanted to go out and work in the field. At the same time Luther hoped he could soon go to Europe to study. They agreed they would each try to obtain a year's fellowship, a scholarship for the support of graduate students. They dreamed of meeting in Europe, at the end of their year's separation, and traveling home together.

Margaret wanted to study the changes that take place in a people's culture. And she wanted to work among the Polynesians, the inhabitants of many islands in the central and southern waters of the Pacific. In fact, she had set her heart on working among the particular group of Polynesians whose home was the remote French-controlled Tuamotu Islands in the South Seas.

She presented her plan to Professor Boas, whose approval she needed in order to win a fellowship. He didn't approve of either her choice of place or choice of subject.

He said her health might be ruined in the tropical Tuamotus. He wanted her to work instead in the United States.

He also said enough studies had already been done on changes in cultures. The time had come, he said, to move on to other things, to other problems. Now he wanted his students to explore the way certain human beings developed in a primitive culture. He had sent one woman student to learn how artists lived and worked in the Zuñi Indian culture. He wanted Margaret to learn about Indian teenage girls, or adolescents. Did they have the same problems American white girls had when they were growing up and their bodies were changing? Did they too become restless and easily upset? Did they rebel against their parents?

Margaret agreed that it would be interesting to study young girls, but she didn't want to give up the rest of her plan.

Of course, it would cost her less to work in the United States, since she would have to pay her own way to the location of her field work. But she told her father that Professor Boas was trying to make her do something she didn't want to do, and Professor Mead didn't like the idea of another man controlling his daughter. So he promised her that if she won her struggle to get to the South Seas, he would pay her fare there, and back home by way of Europe. Margaret was then ready to take up her argument once more.

"Couldn't I study the adolescents of the Tuamotu Polynesians?" she asked.

Professor Boas was a wise man. He knew Margaret would work best in a place where she wanted to be. But he was also stubborn, and he was concerned about her safety.

"The Tuamotu Islands are too remote," he told her. "Ships very seldom visit them. The people there are cut off from the rest of the world for months at a time. So, if you were to get sick there, you couldn't have the care you would need."

"Would you approve of some part of the South Seas that ships do visit regularly?" Margaret asked.

The professor admitted, not very happily, that he could not object to such a place.

"Then I can go to the American-governed Samoan Islands!" Margaret said. "Ships call there every six weeks. Its naval base even has a hospital, so I'd be looked after if I got sick."

And so it was settled. They had both compromised, but Margaret felt she had won most of what she wanted. The Samoan Islands were in the South Seas and their inhabitants were Polynesians.

17

Missionaries had converted the Samoans to Christianity more than a century before, and set down their language in a written form that English-speaking people could read. But the Samoans still clung to most of their ancient ways, and the American authorities were not trying to change them. So in Samoa, Margaret felt sure, she would be living and working among the kind of primitive people she was so eager to know.

Now events moved quickly.

Luther received his fellowship. Margaret received hers too. It would give her $150 a month for a year.

At the end of the summer of 1925 Margaret and Luther had a whole week's vacation together in a borrowed house. They shared a farewell dinner with her family. Then everyone went with her to the Philadelphia railroad station.

Margaret hugged her grandmother, her parents, her brother and her two sisters. She stood on tiptoe for Luther's good-bye kiss. She promised to write to them about everything that happened to her, so she wouldn't seem a stranger when she returned. Then she picked up her bags and walked through the passenger gate and onto the waiting train.

"She never looked back!" her father said.

3/ Talofa Means "Love to Thee"

Margaret seemed very brave that day, setting off alone on a journey halfway around the world. She said, long afterward, that her courage grew out of "almost complete ignorance."

She had no idea what it would be like to do field work. She did know that a Hawaii-born college friend of her mother would meet her when she stopped at Honolulu before sailing on to Samoa. She also knew that the Surgeon General of the United States—an old friend of Luther's father—had asked the U.S. Navy medical branch to help her in Samoa. So her only fear, as her trip began, was that well-meaning people might look after her too well, and leave her no freedom to work.

In Honolulu her mother's friend did insist that Margaret stay at her home. But after introducing her to the very people she most wanted to meet, Margaret's hostess left her completely on her own for her two weeks' stay.

At Honolulu's Bishop Museum the director himself showed her its famous Polynesian collections—woven mats, baskets of many kinds, and beautifully patterned *tapa,* a papery fabric made of tree bark.

Breadfruit

Tapa had been the Polynesians' only cloth until Europeans brought cotton to their islands.

A botanist drove her into the hills above the modern city and taught her to recognize the tropical plants she would see in Samoa—the breadfruit tree, the taro plant with leaves like elephant ears, and the pandanus plant, whose leaves were used for weaving.

A language expert gave her lessons in one of the Polynesian languages related to Samoan.

"I feel as if I've made a start," her letter home added.

The last part of her journey, through the South Seas she had long dreamed of, was the most unpleasant part of her trip. The ship she traveled on was small, and rolled so heavily through the rough Pacific that Margaret couldn't even write a letter. But finally the vessel neared

taro plant

V.J.79

PANDANUS

roots

Tutuila, largest of the American Samoan Islands. And early on a hot sticky morning her captain dropped anchor at the island's chief port, Pago Pago. Margaret had already learned to pronounce that name *pango-pango*, as the Samoans did.

Pago Pago's little harbor had once been the crater of a volcano, and its steep tree-clad sides rose almost straight out of the sea. It looked just like the pictures Margaret had seen of it—except that in those pictures there had been no flag-decked American warships.

"The United States Navy's Pacific fleet is here!" she heard a member of the ship's crew shout.

Margaret knew that about one hundred navy men and their families lived in Pago Pago. The naval officer serving as Samoa's American governor also resided there. She planned to call on him, and to be as polite as necessary to the rest of the town's *papalagi,* as Samoans called white people. But she hoped she could ignore all papalagi most of the time, so that she could concentrate on the first job she had to do: learn the Samoan language.

She realized as soon as she stepped ashore, however, that she couldn't ignore the visiting fleet. It had taken over the town. Pago Pago's little market square was crowded with sailors eager to buy curios from barefoot Samoans. Margaret found a room in Pago Pago's ramshackle hotel, near the end of its one paved street, and told herself to be patient.

The curio sellers were the first Samoans Margaret had seen. They were "too muscular to be pretty, but most magnificent," she wrote in her next letter home. But they were not wearing the handsome lavalavas she had expected to see. Most of the women were in shapeless cotton dresses. The men had added "foreign" shirts to their wraparound skirts made, she reported sadly, of "hideous striped American stuffs."

Only the Samoan chiefs, arriving with ceremonial gifts for the fleet commander, were splendid in native dress. They wore tall headdresses and elaborate grass skirts. The bronze skin of their naked upper bodies had been oiled until it glowed.

Margaret wished she could speak to them in their own tongue. But she didn't see how she could even begin to search for a language teacher until the warships had departed.

Then, before the end of her first day ashore, she was visited by Miss Hodgson, the briskly sensible director of the local training school for native nurses. Miss Hodgson was offering Margaret her help, she said, at the request of the Surgeon General. And she invited Margaret to store

22

her best dresses in Miss Hodgson's own closet, kept dry by a constantly burning electric bulb.

"Otherwise," Miss Hodgson explained kindly, "they will rot or get rust stains from cockroach bites."

Margaret accepted the invitation gratefully, and then told Miss Hodgson about the problem that worried her far more than the hotel's damp closets. To her happy amazement Miss Hodgson soon had a solution to that too. She said she had assigned a native nurse to Margaret for an hour each day, to teach her Samoan.

"Her name is Pepe," Miss Hodgson said. "She comes from a chiefly family and speaks excellent English. There will, of course, be no charge for the lessons, and they can begin as soon as the fleet has departed."

It was almost too good to be true, Margaret thought. She refused to be discouraged even by the words of the elderly naval-officer governor.

"I haven't learned Samoan," he said. "None of the naval men here learn it. You won't either."

On the afternoon of her first lesson, with Pago Pago suddenly silent and empty, Margaret walked to the hospital. Pepe, young and pretty in her nurse's uniform, was waiting for her. Margaret had brought a notebook and freshly sharpened pencils.

"*Talofa,*" Pepe said, smiling. "That is our Samoan greeting," she explained. "The word really means 'Love to thee,' but we use it when English-speaking people would say 'Good morning' or 'Good evening.' "

"Talofa," Margaret repeated, and then wrote the word down, just as it had sounded to her, putting an accent mark on the syllable Pepe had accented. "Talofa," she said again, trying to make her voice rise and fall musically, to "sing" the word as Pepe had.

Pepe nodded approval. "And the reply to that greeting is 'Love to thee, indeed,' *Talofa lava*," she said.

The hour went quickly. Margaret wrote down everything Pepe dictated to her, and then spoke the words aloud, sometimes repeating a phrase several times before it was correct. Later, back in her own room, she went over all the words and phrases until she knew them by heart.

The next morning she opened the Samoan-English dictionary Christian missionaries had prepared years before, and began to memorize words from its pages.

Afafine meant daughter, she learned—and then discovered that the word was used only by a man. A woman spoke of her daughter as her *tama*.

At the end of the morning's work she went downstairs for lunch. Now that the fleet had left, she was the hotel's only guest. And the cook (Margaret had already discovered he wasn't very good at his job) had prepared only Samoan food. She was served octopus soup, a roasted wild pigeon, and a large slice of cooked taro root that resembled a cake of gray soap. Margaret thought the taro tasted like putty, but she knew she would have to get used to it. Taro was a part of almost every Samoan meal. She finished the whole big slice.

During the stifling heat of early afternoon all Pago Pago slept. Margaret was determined to study instead. She meant to put in a full day's work every day in return for her $150 monthly check. Back in her room once more, after lunch, she sat down again with her dictionary.

But within a few minutes she began to feel dizzy. The printed page blurred before her eyes. The dizziness grew worse and she felt as if she could scarcely breathe the oven-like air, heavy with the smell of frangipani blossoms and overripe bananas.

Shakily she moved to her bed, remembering what she had heard about tropical diseases and their victims.

"Margaret won't be able to resist those diseases. She ought to forget the idea of trying to do field work in the tropics." That's what several people at home had said. Now for the first time she was afraid they might have been right.

It was late in the day when she woke from the heavy sleep she had fallen into. A cooling breeze drifted through the room.

"But I feel perfectly well!" she told herself in amazement.

Then she became aware of that breeze and knew what it meant.

She knew that her spell of dizzy sickness had been brought on by the midday heat and her stubborn insistence on trying to work through it.

It was too bad, she thought, but she wouldn't dare do that again. She had had her first important lesson since leaving home and she had to accept it. From now on she too would rest every day in the early afternoon.

Vai Togi

Chief Ufuti

4/ Visit to Vaitogi

"Steamer day" made the one dramatic break in Margaret's program after she had been in Pago Pago for three weeks. The steamship brought the first mail she had received since she'd left Honolulu. She spread her fifty-eight letters out on her bed and felt "half sick with excitement," she wrote her family later.

Every day, as she walked through the town after her lesson with Pepe, she said "Talofa" to the Samoans she passed.

"Talofa lava," most people replied, smiling at the white girl who was trying to learn their language.

But one day Margaret added a whole sentence to her greeting—her Samoan translation of "The Samoan language is very difficult." And that day people simply stared at her and looked puzzled. She tried the same sentence the next day and the next. They still stared. Finally she learned that by placing one accent in the wrong place, she had actually been saying, "The Samoan language is very vaccination!"

She began to wonder how much of this difficult language she could learn in the six weeks she planned to spend in Pago Pago before moving to a village to start her real field work. She was also worried about where that work should be done.

"Could you recommend a village where I might work?" she asked a naval officer. "It should be the sort of place where Samoans still live the way they used to—a place that hasn't been much changed by our papalagi customs."

"But you can't possibly live in that sort of village!" he said. "You couldn't live in a native hut or live on a diet of native food."

Every navy man she talked to agreed with him.

"All the natives want to wear glasses, and would steal yours while you're asleep!" one added.

Then a navy doctor took her along on one of his two-day inspection trips into the island's interior. It was her "first real *malaga* (journey)," she reported to her family. She and the doctor and his wife had gone on foot, she wrote, over a steep mountain trail. A *fitafita,* a member of the native marine corps, carried their supplies in large palm leaf baskets hung from a pole balanced over his shoulder.

For the first time Margaret saw some of the villages more than a few miles distant from Pago Pago. Each was a cluster of open-walled thatch-roofed buildings. In each she and her friends were entertained in the guest house every chief kept ready for visitors.

Each visit began with the Samoans' traditional food offering and gift-exchange ceremony called *ta'alolo*. Margaret, like the doctor's wife, received delicate shell necklaces. In one village she was also presented with a beautifully decorated kava cup. She was embarrassed by the gifts she and her companions gave in return—cigars for the men and chewing gum for their wives. But the doctor assured her that was just what the Samoans wanted.

A dance ceremony, or *siva*, was staged in their honor in each village. And at every visit's end they drank the ceremonial kava served by the chief's ceremonial princess, his taupou, who was usually his oldest unmarried daughter.

After that journey Margaret realized she couldn't live in one of those villages for many months, after all. Samoan custom would make it impossible for her to have a house of her own. To live with a native family, in a house without walls, would leave her no privacy at all. And though she enjoyed many Samoan dishes, a steady Samoan diet would be too starchy for her to digest.

Where then could she do her field work? The question troubled her more each day. If she stayed near the naval station, she could get the food she needed, but she wouldn't be able to meet the "old-fashioned" Samoan girls she wanted to study.

Her problem was finally solved by Ruth Holt, a young white woman who had come to Pago Pago's naval hospital to await the birth of her second child. Ruth Holt's husband was a chief pharmacist's mate in charge of the navy's medical station on the island of Tau, a hundred miles from the island of Tutuila. The Holts, their two-year-old son, and two enlisted men who served as radio operators were Tau's only white people.

"You could stay with us," Mrs. Holt offered. "We live in the dispensary. It's the only papalagi building on the island. And we buy supplies from the navy commissary here, so our meals are mostly

American food. But in the three villages close to the dispensary you'd find dozens of really old-fashioned Samoan girls to study."

And so it was settled. Margaret would go to Tau as soon as Ruth Holt and her new baby were ready to travel.

While she waited, she was invited to visit the village of Vaitogi as the guest of Chief Ufuti. He had heard of Margaret through one of his relatives, a woman Margaret had met, and he was curious about her. Margaret was curious about him too. He was known as one of the most intelligent chiefs on Tutuila. And his village, some twelve miles from Pago Pago, was said to be very beautiful.

In Vaitogi Margaret would have to speak Samoan all day every day, and she knew how helpful that would be. She asked Pepe to prepare her for the visit by teaching her the proper way to greet a chief and "she who sits in the back of the house," as a chief's wife was called. Then, with great care, she chose the gifts she would bring her hosts—cloth for lavalavas for the chief and his wife, and perfume for their daughter, Fa'amotu.

Margaret spent her ten-day visit in the chief's own home, since his guest house was occupied by a visiting chief and his staff. She was called Makelita, the Samoan version of Margaret, and the title of taupou which the chief gave her made her an honorary member of his family. (A Samoan taupou was always an unmarried girl, but Margaret had not let it be known that she was married; she wanted to appear as much as possible like the young girls she was going to study.)

A deep pile of mats was prepared for her to sleep on, beside her new "sister," Fa'amotu. A mosquito netting was let down around their beds each night, its corners held in place by small stones. It was needed to keep out insects and wandering dogs, chickens, and pigs.

Each morning at dawn she was wakened by Fa'amotu's soft whisper. "It is morning, Makelita," Fa'amotu said in Samoan.

Together then, each wrapped in her own sheet, they walked barefoot to the beach to bathe in the surf. Afterward Margaret sat cross-legged on a mat, eating her breakfast with her fingers. As an honored guest, she was served before anyone else in the family ate.

Every day she was given lessons in Samoan etiquette by Lolo, talking chief of the visiting chief. The most important things he taught her were the special words a Samoan should use when addressing a chief, and the different special words used when speaking with talking chiefs. Lolo and Ufuti were both proud of her progress, and her successful serving during the kava-drinking ceremony delighted them. All the men of the village joined them in honoring her with a ceremonial dance. She was the first white woman they had ever known who wanted to learn their language and all their traditional ways.

Margaret worked hard over the farewell speech she knew she was expected to make before her departure. In her best Samoan, on the day she left, she said she would still remember her visit to Vaitogi when she was "old and bent and wrinkled." Everyone in the village applauded.

"I never spent a more peacefully happy and comfortable ten days in my life," Margaret's letter home said.

But the young girls of Vaitogi, in awe of her because she was a taupou, had avoided her in spite of her efforts to be friendly. The same thing would happen, she realized, in any village where she was a chief's honored guest. So she decided that while she stayed with the Holts she must not only appear as an unmarried girl; she must also avoid invitations from chiefly families.

She had learned a lot during her Vaitogi visit. Her Samoan was much improved. From now on, if she could convince young girls to talk with her, she felt sure her field work would go well. One advantage she knew she possessed was her height—only a few inches over five feet. She was no taller than most Samoan girls in their teens.

Margaret was therefore full of confidence on the early November day when a naval vessel took her and Ruth Holt and the new baby to the island of Tau.

Margaret Mead
and Fa'amatu
in Samoa

5/ Tua and Ula Talk to Makelita

Late in the morning of her first day on Tau Margaret finished tacking up her photographs of everyone she felt close to. They made her feel less lonely in this room where she would spend the next six months.

It was scarcely an ordinary room. It was half of the screened rear porch of the dispensary, a building with green painted walls and a corrugated iron roof. Margaret could pull a curtain across the middle of the space to divide it in two. Her bed had been set up on one side of that curtain, her table on the other. On the table, which she would use as her desk, were her field work supplies—a small camera, six fat notebooks, a portable typewriter, pencils, and stacks of paper. A loosely woven bamboo screen walled off her half of the porch from the half used by the dispensary patients.

There were no patients now, but beyond the screen Margaret saw two small girls, each carrying a smaller child on her hip. Silently they drew nearer until they could peer between the bamboo slats. The flowers tucked behind their ears had wilted. The loose blouses they wore over their lavalavas stuck damply to their shoulders. But their eyes were bright with curiosity.

"Talofa," Margaret greeted them politely.

"Talofa lava," they both said, and giggled.

They were no more than seven or eight years old, Margaret thought. But if she hoped to understand adolescents, she knew she must learn about the younger girls who would become adolescents someday.

She invited them into her room and they entered shyly, still giggling. Immediately they seated their small charges on the floor, and sat cross-legged beside them. Margaret sat down too. Samoans always sat cross-legged on the floor inside a house, whatever they happened to be doing.

"My name is Makelita," Margaret said. "What are your names?"

"Tua," one said.

"Ula," said the other.

"How old are you?" Margaret asked.

The question seemed to puzzle the girls.

"I am younger than my big brother and four sisters," Tua said after a pause. "But I am older than this brother," and she looked down at the child beside her.

Ula answered the same way. She was younger than one sister and one brother, but older than another brother and two other sisters.

"When is your day of birth?" Margaret asked. She didn't know the Samoan word for "birthday."

Again the girls seemed puzzled. Neither answered her.

But a moment later Ula began to tell her proudly about watching the birth of her mother's newest baby. Many people had come to her house that night, she said. They had stayed until dawn, when the baby finally arrived. And there had been much to eat and drink.

"When was the baby born?" Margaret asked.

Ula thought the baby had come before the breadfruit was ripe, but she wasn't really sure.

Ula and Tua had given Margaret her first hint of an important fact she would soon record in her notebooks: the birth of a Samoan child was an important event, but its date was soon forgotten. Samoan children therefore never knew exactly how old they were. What they did know was their place in the family order. And they were brought up to obey those older than themselves, and to take care of those who were younger.

Tua's little brother was trying to struggle to his feet. Tua spoke sharply to him and pulled him down again.

Margaret wished she could suggest that he be allowed to stand up and move about, but she knew Tua was doing her best to teach him proper behavior. A Samoan child who stood in the presence of his elders was not showing the proper respect.

"Who is the old white man in the picture?" Ula asked. She had been staring curiously around the room.

"My teacher, Professor Boas," Margaret told her.

"Who are these people?" Ula asked next, and Margaret said they were her parents.

When she had explained all her pictures to them—carefully omitting to say that Luther was her husband—Ula had another question.

"Do you like to swim, Makelita?"

"I like it very much," Margaret said.

Ula then described to her their special swimming hole among the big rocks along the shore. Water poured quickly into that hole through a narrow opening, with every incoming wave. It drained out just as quickly when the wave fell back.

"It makes us jump up and down!" Tua said. "We call it our jumping hole."

A voice from inside the dispensary interrupted them. Mr. Holt was calling out to Margaret that lunch was ready.

"My *matai* is calling me," Margaret told the girls, using the Samoan word for the head of a household.

The girls immediately got to their feet, ready to leave. They were taking for granted that Margaret would obey her matai instantly, just as they obeyed their own. It meant they really were accepting her as someone much like themselves, Margaret thought. She wanted to hug them.

Ula turned back for one last word. "We could take you to our jumping hole tomorrow," she said.

"I would like that," Margaret told them.

But the next morning she woke up with a throat so painfully sore that she couldn't speak.

Mr. Holt examined her and took her temperature. "Tonsillitis," he said. "A really bad attack. Get back to bed and stay there. I'll send Ruth to you with some medicine."

Left alone in her porch room, a little later, Margaret told herself feverishly, "But I can't be sick! I mustn't be! I have to work!"

She thought of all the things she should be doing. So far she had explored Luma, the village surrounding the dispensary, only briefly.

She had had even less time for its neighboring village of Siufaga. And she had not been near the third village of Faleasao, half a mile away along the shore.

She wished there were someone beside the well-meaning Holts she could talk to—someone who would understand why an anthropologist could not afford to miss a single day's work. She wished it didn't feel as if a knife were being stabbed into her throat each time she swallowed.

She had never felt so miserable and alone in all her life. She had to squeeze her eyes tightly to keep back the tears.

6/ Growing Up in Samoa

A long week went by before Margaret was able to be out of bed. But during that week she discovered she could learn a good deal by listening to sounds, sniffing the air, and talking to the young village girl who helped take care of two-year-old Arthur Holt.

Early each morning, for example, Margaret had smelled smoke through the usual scents of flowers and bananas. She knew now that it came from the several fires being built in round stone pits. A single fire was used by a whole household—and a household might consist of as many as four families, adding up to twenty people or more. Tended by the boys and young men who did most of the village cooking, a fire was kept burning until the stones were white hot. Then the ashes were removed and the pits were filled with enough food for three or four days—bananas, yams, and leaf-wrapped chickens and chunks of pork and fish. Finally everything was covered with green leaves and left to bake. The members of a household had a hot meal only on what Samoans called "the day the oven was opened." The rest of the time they ate their food cold.

The shouts that Margaret heard sometimes at dawn, just as the roosters were crowing, came from some of the older boys. They were waking their friends for a fishing expedition.

And she could now understand the rhythmic banging of wood on wood which came later in the day. It signaled the men and most of the older boys—and sometimes older girls and women too—to gather at the village center with their digging sticks. Then they would climb five miles inland to the plantation that the whole village farmed together. There they raised the taro, yams, and bananas that formed the largest part of their diet.

At the end of the day, when the plantation workers returned, a matai's voice could be heard as he distributed his household's share of the harvest.

And the triumphant shouts that sometimes woke Margaret from a deep sleep, late in the afternoon, meant the fishermen were returning with a good catch. Afterward she lay listening to the booming voice of a talking chief, calling out the cup-names of the men being served their kava.

If she heard singing in the evening, accompanied by guitars and ukuleles and the clapping of hands, that meant that somewhere the young people were dancing. Often the village did not fall silent until midnight.

Margaret had a visitor when she was well again. He was the native pastor of the village church, and he kept a boarding school in his home for some of the island girls. He brought one of his students with him.

"This is Felofiaina," he told Margaret. "She is one of my good

Christian girls. She can read and write Samoan and will be useful in your work."

Margaret wasn't surprised that he seemed to know all about her. News spread quickly in a Samoan village. She welcomed the shy young girl, who seemed about twelve years old, and told the pastor she was grateful. When the villagers realized that he trusted one of his students to her, she thought, they probably would be willing for their own girls to spend time with her too.

Margaret took Felofiaina for a walk that day. She wanted to make a map showing every building in the three neighboring villages. Then she would learn the number of girls in each house, how the members of a family were related to each other, and how each family was related to other families.

First she stood in front of the dispensary and drew a square in her notebook to represent that building. Close to it she drew a circle for the small Samoan-style house in front of the dispensary. She had been told she could use that house for her meetings with the village young people.

Ula and Tua appeared as she finished, each once more with a baby on her hip. During a polite conversation about Margaret's illness, the girls were called by some distant grown-up. Quickly they asked if Margaret still wanted to visit their jumping hole, and she promised to go with them the following day. Then they ran off obediently with their heavy burdens.

Next Margaret drew squares for the buildings nearby. One was for the little store where an energetic Samoan sold cloth, paper, kerosene for lamps, and a few dishes. Another was for the warehouse where the villagers stored the dried coconut meat called copra. Margaret knew that selling copra to the government and making souvenirs to sell to the navy men in Pago Pago were the only ways most villagers could earn money. Most things the Samoans needed, of course, they grew or made for themselves.

Finally, with Felofiaina beside her, Margaret started along the sandy seaside path that ran the length of Luma and Siufaga. The rows of coconut palms on each side of it had been planted only ten years earlier, Mr. Holt had said, after a hurricane destroyed all the villagers' houses and the palm trees then growing around them.

Above their heads a little girl was walking up one of the slanted trunks. Felofiaina urged Margaret to hurry, so they wouldn't be struck by one of the coconuts the girl was about to throw down.

At each of the houses scattered along the path Margaret stopped to draw another square, and to greet anyone in sight.

In one yard a mother sat cross-legged on the bare earth, nursing her baby. A girl about eight years old watched over a tiny boy who suddenly toddled toward Margaret and grabbed at her skirt. The mother turned angrily on the girl, who snatched up the baby and hurried off with him.

It seemed to Margaret that young Samoan girls were like little slaves, burdened by the responsibility of the babies and sternly ruled by their elders.

At another house a woman was weaving four large palm leaves into a *fala*, a simple floor mat. Beside her a young woman, clearly her tama or daughter, was weaving golden-white thread-like strands into the special kind of mat that was part of every Samoan girl's marriage dowry. Such a mat, as soft and fine as linen, might take a year or more to make. Margaret asked the weaver if hers would be finished soon.

"No," the young woman said, and laughed. "I do not hurry."

Samoan marriage, Margaret would soon understand, was a sober affair decided upon with the advice of both families. A young woman might fall in love several times, but she thought of those adventures as part of the freedom of being unmarried. And she enjoyed that freedom so much that she wasn't eager to exchange it for the responsibilities of a wife and mother.

Margaret finished her map of Luma with a square for the white-walled thatch-roofed church. The house on its far side was the first house in Siufaga. But now it was noon and too hot to stay outdoors.

Gradually Margaret learned a great deal about the inhabitants of her three villages. There were less than a thousand of them altogether— about three hundred in each village. And among the young people there was frequent shifting from one house to another. Girls who were unhappy at home for any reason often left to stay with relatives. Or a girl with no small brother or sister to look after might be "borrowed" by a relative who needed a baby-sitter.

Finally Margaret was ready to make a list of the fifty girls she had decided to study most closely. Their ages began at about seven. The oldest were nineteen or twenty.

Most of the girls, and a good many boys as well, had become her friends by then. She went swimming with them in the jumping hole, where the surging waves lifted her up as much as ten feet, and dropped her swiftly down again. On Sunday she joined them in church, and sang

hymns that had been translated into Samoan. With the older girls she made the long uphill journey to the village plantation. And boys and girls came to the dispensary porch morning, afternoon, and evening, in search of Makelita.

The small girls like Tua and Ula usually came singly or in pairs, never without the babies that were put in their charge as soon as they were weaned.

Girls about ten or more usually came in giggling groups. They had younger sisters old enough to take over the day-long task of caring for smaller children, so they were free to play for part of the day. But they were also learning women's work—weaving of many kinds, a little

44

cooking, how to choose ripe fruit, how to select exactly the right leaves for mats and baskets. Most of them also learned how to prepare mulberry bark for the tapa cloth still used for ceremonial lavalavas. Margaret often joined them at their lessons.

The teenagers—by this time they were joined by boys—came mostly in the evenings, after the day's fishing and farming were done. They looked at the magazines Margaret's friends had sent her. They teased each other and called on Margaret to take sides in their arguments.

"She wants to go home to see her sweetheart," one boy said of a visiting girl.

"He's a liar!" the girl said. "I have no sweetheart!"

"She's a liar! She has many!" the boy said, and then turned to Margaret. "Makelita, ask her how many sweethearts she has."

Always Margaret listened. And she watched them when they danced. All the young Samoans danced. They tied siva skirts over their lavalavas. They put flowers behind their ears. Necklaces of seeds or shells or blossoms or colored paper bounced on the girls' blouses and around their ankles, and on the boys' bare chests. Each performance was a solo, with no set pattern of steps. Each dancer tried to outdo all the others.

But girls didn't try to outdo others in the grown-up skills they were learning, Margaret discovered. Any girl who did that would be told she was showing off. Her elders had a special way of scolding her.

"You are presuming above your age," they said.

Even a poor weaver could explain her lack of skill by saying simply, "I am but young." Nobody made her feel ashamed. It was taken for granted that she would learn to weave well enough eventually. Weaving wasn't difficult. In fact, few of the tasks a Samoan girl would face as a grown-up were difficult to perform.

Margaret was also learning that Samoan girls were growing up in a world where people seldom hurried. They didn't have to. Samoans worked only long enough each day to supply themselves with the few things they needed for their way of life. The rest of the time they could relax and enjoy themselves—visiting, feasting, and dancing. And they expected to go on just as they were, with each new generation living as the one before it had lived.

It was a world very different from the one Margaret had left behind.

7/ New Year's Celebration and Catastrophe

The weeks went by and suddenly Christmas was only days away. Its celebration was one Christian custom the Samoans had adopted with special enthusiasm. All the talk was now about gifts.

Girls came to Margaret's porch, or the little Samoan house near the dispensary, with seeds and shells. Hour after hour they sat stringing them into necklaces. The Holts worried over the cost of the 150 presents they would be expected to distribute. Margaret stretched her scant funds to buy cloth for her more important gifts, and ordered dozens of less expensive things from the navy commissary.

She spent the whole day before Christmas wrapping little packages—a comb and a mirror in one, a mirror and a bar of soap in another. Her wrapping paper was brightly colored so that it could be used to make a paper necklace. Her packages were fastened with rubber bands because the Samoans treasured them.

Gift givers had started arriving early that morning. By evening, she wrote her family, "the traffic was fast and furious." It went on all Christmas Day.

Margaret received countless necklaces. She put on the first ones until she was wearing half a dozen. Then she took those off and hung them over her curtain wire so that she could wear the next half dozen she was given. But the fragile necklaces kept coming. Finally, her letter home said, she had hung so many on the wire that they "made a curtain of themselves and every visitor stopped to admire them."

By then her table was piled high with mats, fans, lengths of tapa cloth, siva skirts, and the other gifts she had received.

"Each visitor wanted to know who had given me what till my head reeled," her letter said.

Preparations for the New Year's holiday—an even more important occasion in Samoa—began as soon as Christmas was over. There would be feasting on New Year's Day, but the celebration would begin the night before.

The great evening arrived with a burst of noise. As Margaret walked along the beach with an excited group of girls, everyone was shouting out greetings for the New Year and dozens of boys were beating the tin cans they had hung around their necks. *Bang! Bang! Bang!* The loud steady beat never faltered.

"They can make a noise louder than thunder!" one girl said proudly.

"Yes, they can," Margaret agreed, hands over her ears.

The deafening beat was still pounding her eardrums when she dropped into bed long after midnight.

But she roused herself early the next morning. She wanted to watch the villagers gather for the traditional New Year's feasting and dancing. In family groups the Samoans left their homes, dressed in their best.

Then it began to rain, and powerful sand-laden gusts of wind swept down the hill behind the village.

Holiday clothes were drenched in an instant. Paper necklaces were whipped into sodden shreds. The villagers turned and ran through the torrent toward their homes, to find shelter behind hastily lowered blinds.

Tropical storms were often brief. Margaret waited restlessly for this one to end. Instead it grew steadily worse. By midafternoon it had reached hurricane force.

Margaret remembered the stories she'd been told about the disastrous hurricane of ten years before. Mrs. Holt, her baby held close in her arms, remembered them too.

"As long as the wind comes from behind us, we'll be all right," Mr. Holt said. He had to raise his voice to be heard. The dispensary's metal roof sheets were being lifted by the wind and slammed noisily down again. The roof was already leaking in half a dozen places.

The Holts and a young radio operator joined Margaret at a window. Together they stared at a thatched roof nearby as it rocked back and forth with each new blast of the gale. It collapsed as they watched it, and portions of thatch sailed through the air.

Within minutes several other buildings went down in the same way.

And then the wind stopped, as if it had been turned off. Palm leaves no longer waved wildly. Nothing stirred. The heat of the motionless air was suffocating.

That breathless stillness, Mr. Holt said grimly, meant that the eye of the hurricane was passing overhead. It lasted only a few moments. Then the full fury of the wind struck again, this time sweeping in from the sea.

From then on things happened quickly. Coconuts and tree branches hurtled past like projectiles. Sheets of metal from the dispensary roof were carried away. The cracking of timbers and the shattering of glass announced that the whole front porch of the building had been ripped loose. The building's seaward door, left unprotected, blew inward and admitted the storm's full force.

Margaret and the others retreated swiftly to the dining room at the rear of the building. For a moment, at least, they were safe there. But Mr. Holt was worried. He and the radio operator disappeared into the howling darkness outside.

Margaret looked around for flashlights, candles, and matches. Mrs. Holt was collecting blankets and sweaters for the children.

The men reappeared. "Come along," Mr. Holt said. "We've drained most of the water out of the water tank, and put things in it to sit on. We'll stay there until it's over."

Clinging to each other, heads down, they made their way into the yard. The water tank was a concrete structure some five feet square and just about as high. Its metal cover had been pulled back to make an opening barely large enough for a person to squeeze through.

"You go first, Margaret," Mr. Holt said.

He helped her climb over the tank's wall. She lowered herself on the other side into utter darkness and several inches of water. Her flashlight showed several wooden boxes and the big dishpan the men had brought from the house.

"Take the baby's washtub," Mr. Holt was saying, and handed it down to her. "And here's the baby. She's upside down!" he warned.

Margaret reached up for the blanket-wrapped bundle, felt for the baby's head, and lowered her into the tub.

"And here comes Arthur," Mr. Holt called.

Margaret took the two-year-old and sat him down on the overturned dishpan. Then she held the baby with one hand and Arthur with the other, until Mrs. Holt joined her. The radio operator came next. And finally Mr. Holt dropped into the tank with a loaf of bread and a roasted chicken.

For hours the wind howled over them as they huddled inside the tank. Their feet were wet and cold in the water on the floor. The rain poured in through the half-opened top to soak them from above. They gave Arthur a chicken leg to chew on. He cried until he fell asleep.

Not long before sunrise Margaret realized that the wind and the rain were easing. A few moments later both stopped and all was still again.

The hurricane was over.

Wearily, their muscles aching, Margaret and the others climbed out of their makeshift shelter into a strangely quiet world.

Only the rear of the dispensary—the part of the building, fortunately, where Margaret's records were stored—was still standing. All but five of the other houses in Luma had been completely destroyed by the New Year's Day catastrophe.

Rebuilding after a hurricane

8/ Margaret Takes Stock

Cleaning up after the hurricane, and rebuilding the villages, was a big job. A navy ship brought workmen and materials for repairing the dispensary. It also brought Red Cross food supplies for the Holt household and for the villagers whose crops had been destroyed. Everyone lived on canned salmon and rice, and worked from dawn to dark.

While Samoan men and boys put up new houses, Margaret helped the women and girls who were weaving the new blinds they all needed. Soon the Samoan grown-ups stopped thinking of her as that strange white woman who spent so much time with their children. By the time life was normal again Makelita had become part of their adult community.

This meant that from then on they invited her to share important events like the roasted-pig feast that celebrated a baby's birth. They did favors for her and, according to Samoan custom, expected favors in return. Mostly they wanted Makelita to take pictures of themselves and their relatives. Once, Margaret wrote home, she was asked to walk half a mile to Faleasao, the farthest village, "on the hottest day we've ever had and take a picture of a corpse."

Now the young people were free to visit her again. Small girls arrived outside her porch as early as five o'clock in the morning. Older ones came late in the evening, with flaming torches, begging her to join an adventurous night fishing trip. Her visitors left her no time to study the vast amount of material she had been gathering.

She was sure she had found the answer to Professor Boas's questions about the adolescent girls in Samoa. The answer was that they had almost none of the difficulties American girls usually had at that age.

"The adolescent years," Margaret would write later, "were the best years of a Samoan girl's life."

She believed the reason for this was the way the girls were brought up in the Samoan culture. But until she had gone through her notebooks, she wouldn't know if she had enough facts to defend that belief against any scientists who might question it. Every day she hoped for time to take stock, as she put it. She kept remembering, as she wrote home, that her work might be cut short any day "by illness or hurricane or what not."

Finally, one rainy day, she was left alone long enough to do what she wished. By late that night she could feel that she had already accomplished a great deal.

Her notes clearly showed the reasons why a Samoan girl's upbringing led to an adolescence of few difficulties. Some of those reasons were:

A Samoan girl never felt the deep love for any one person that often led to anxiety for American adolescents. This lack of deep caring for anyone—even for her mother—began as a baby when she was handed casually around among her older sisters and all the women of the village.

As a young girl she didn't have just one "best friend" among the girls she knew. Usually, instead, all or most of the girls in a single village formed a loose group of casual friends.

When she was older, the Samoan girl was in some ways just as casual about the boys of the village. She knew her parents wouldn't object if she had a few love affairs before her carefully planned marriage. They thought it was only natural, since in their unwalled house she had seen and learned all about adult lovemaking. (A girl who had many affairs, however, was frowned upon and would probably not be able to make a good marriage.) But there was usually a certain formal ceremony about these love affairs. A young man didn't approach a girl directly. Instead he sent a friend as his "talking chief," to convince the girl he was good and gentle and worthy of her love.

A Samoan girl didn't have to spend unhappy weeks in rebellion against her parents, if she resented their authority in some way. She simply moved away from them and stayed for a time at the home of a relative.

A Samoan girl didn't have to compete with her friends. No one expected her to outdo others of her age or size, or to be superior to them in any way.

A Samoan girl knew just what life would be like for her when she grew up. She knew she would be able to do everything a wife and mother was expected to do. She had no fears about becoming an adult. And so her adolescence was a happy, carefree time between the responsibilities of her early childhood and her future responsibilities as a married woman. In the weeks that followed Margaret's stock-taking, she made visits to two nearby islands and to the village of Fitiuta at the far end of Tau.

Each journey added to the material in her notebooks. On each return the villagers let her know they had missed her, and that they knew she would someday leave and not come back.

"God love you, you are going away!" they said sadly.

Suddenly the adolescent boys and girls who came to sit on her porch were busy writing flowery farewell songs. With great effort they fitted their words to tunes they knew, usually a song they had learned from sailors. "Just Before the Battle, Mother," was one of their favorites.

"Now sing it for me," Margaret always said, when a song was done. And then she invited the author to write the Samoan verse in one of her notebooks.

In June she packed up those notebooks, along with her typewriter and her camera. After almost nine months in Samoa, it was time to leave. For days she had taken part in endless good-bye ceremonies and exchanges of gifts. Now the boat had arrived that would carry her back to Pago Pago on the first part of her long journey home by way of Australia and Europe.

It seemed as if all the villagers on Tau had gathered to see her off. She waved for as long as she could see them.

Often during the past months she had been homesick for family and old friends, for such things as steak, a bath in a real tub, and the privacy of a room with solid walls and a door that could be closed and locked. Now those things would once more be a part of her life.

But as she touched the flower necklaces her new friends had hung around her neck, she thought how sad it was that people didn't wear flower necklaces in America. She would miss them. She would miss being Makelita.

9/ Fame—and More Field Work

Margaret's report on her field work was not written only for scientists. It was written so that everyone could understand it. Late in 1928 it was published as a book, *Coming of Age in Samoa*. The book was an instant success, especially among students and teachers and parents—the people Margaret had kept especially in mind as she wrote.

Most of its readers had probably once believed that, as was often said, "You can't change human nature, and it's human nature for adolescents to be restless and rebellious." From Margaret's book they learned that much of what they had called "human nature" wasn't "natural" at all. Instead, it was the trained behavior of people brought up in a particular culture.

The book also showed them that at least one culture, the Samoan, produced serene, untroubled adolescents. And it showed readers that by learning about Samoan culture—or any culture that seemed strange to them—they could better understand their own, and all their fellow human beings.

Translated into many foreign languages, *Coming of Age in Samoa* helped change people's thinking all over the world.

The book is still popular today, but now it has a preface written in 1973. Margaret Mead wrote that new preface to remind readers that Samoa's culture is no longer simple and primitive, as it was when she first knew it. Today, in fact, if Samoans want to know how their parents and grandparents lived, they read the book Makelita wrote about them.

After Margaret Mead's return from Samoa, doctors had told her that she wouldn't be able to have any children of her own. Luther had decided to leave the ministry. And they had matured in such different directions, during their separation, that they agreed to a divorce. (After a brief second marriage to Reo Fortune, a fellow anthropologist, Margaret married anthropologist Gregory Bateson and, in 1939, she did give birth to a daughter.)

By 1928, when her book about Samoa was published, Margaret was back in the South Pacific, studying young children in the Admiralty Islands. She was doing her first field work for the American Museum of Natural History, whose staff she had joined on her return from Samoa. Her office, high in one of the turrets of that vast museum on New York City's Central Park West, became her headquarters and in many ways her only permanent home.

The pattern of her life was finally set. From then on, except during the years of World War II, she made one field trip after another to the Pacific. On one of them, in 1971, she was joyously welcomed back to Samoa by women who had once called her Makelita and who were, many of them, now grandmothers like herself. Between trips she taught and lectured and wrote more books. And she helped arrange her own collection of mats and baskets, of photographs and other things, for the magnificent exhibit she created for the museum's Hall of the Peoples of the Pacific.

In 1977 the museum celebrated her seventy-fifth birthday with a five-day festival. Anthropologists and other scientists came from every part of the globe to give lectures, show films, and display exhibits, all in Margaret's honor. And Margaret herself lectured and showed some of her own films. She had pioneered in the use of movie film for field work, because she realized how valuable a form of record-keeping it could be.

Thousands of visitors crowded the museum during those five days, to listen and look and wonder. All of them hoped to catch at least a glimpse of the famous Dr. Margaret Mead, tall crook-handled walking stick in hand, as she strode through the museum's corridors or entered a packed auditorium.

Margaret had to fit that remarkable birthday party into a schedule as crowded as it had always been. She had recently returned from one of her field trips. She was about to leave on a lecture tour. Her latest book would soon be published.

Her chief interest was the young people she had been studying for half a century. It was for them she was doing what she and her father had once agreed was the most important thing any human being could do: adding to the world's store of knowledge.

She had already added more than her share to that store. But she believed that while there were still people who didn't understand each other, and who quarreled or went to war over their differences, there was still a great deal more to be done. She couldn't afford to let even a spectacular seventy-fifth birthday celebration really interrupt her work.

And no one who knew her was surprised that she went right on working—traveling, writing, and teaching—until within a few weeks of her death on November 15, 1978. "Death," someone who knew her wrote, "was the only force that could still the indomitable Margaret Mead."

GLOSSARY

AFAFINE   Daughter (man speaking).

FALA   Woven mat.

FALETELE   Chief's guest house.

FALETUA   "She who sits in back of the house"; the courtesy term for a chief's wife.

FITAFITA   A member of the native marine corps.

KAVA   A drink made of shredded root of the kava bush.

LAVALAVA   Wraparound skirt.

MALAGA   Journey; ceremonial visiting party.

MATAI   Head of a household.

PAPALAGI   White men; literally "sky busters."

SIVA   Dance ceremony.

TALOFA   "Love to thee," standard greeting.

TALOFA LAVA   "Love to thee, indeed," reply to "Talofa."

TA'ALOLO   Ceremonial food offering and gift exchange.

TAMA   Daughter (woman speaking).

TAPA   Bark cloth.

TAUPOU   Ceremonial "princess"; the girl whom a chief has honored with a title.

PRONUNCIATION OF VOWELS
a as in *ah*
e as in *ebb*
i as in *it*
o as in *so*
u as in *pull*

SELECTED BIBLIOGRAPHY

Bauer, Carol Church. *Margaret Mead, Student of the Global Village*, Greenhaven Press, 1976.

Mead, Margaret. *Coming of Age in Samoa*, William Morrow & Co., 1928 (new preface, 1973).

——— *Blackberry Winter, My Earlier Years*, William Morrow & Co., 1972.

——— *Letters From the Field, 1925-1975*, Harper & Row, 1977.

——— *Writings of Ruth Benedict: An Anthropologist at Work*, Avon, 1973.

——— "Life as a Samoan Girl," a chapter in *All True, The Record of Actual Adventures That Have Happened to Ten Women of Today*, Brewer, Warren & Putnam, 1931.

Yost, Edna. *American Women of Science*, J. B. Lippincott & Co., 1955.